Nastia Liukin
Ballerina of Gymnastics

GymnStars
VOLUME 2

654321

CREATIVE MEDIA, INC.
PO Box 6270
Whittier, California 90609-6270
United States of America

WWW.CREATIVEMEDIA.NET

Front cover photo by Jasmin Schneebeli-Wochner
Back cover photo by Ricardo Bufolin
Cover and Book design by Joseph Dzidrums

Printed in the United States of America.

First Edition: April 2012

Library of Congress Control Number: 2012905351

ISBN 978-1-938438-00-4   10 9 8 7

Nastia Liukin
Ballerina of Gymnastics

GymnStars
VOLUME 2

A Biography by
Christine Dzidrums

Special thanks to:
Ricardo Bufolin
Joseph Dzidrums
Amy Jeanius
Jamie Lantzy
Christopher Longoria
Caroline Martin
Pam Mayer
Jeffrey Poulter
Love to:
Joshua, Timothy and Carmel

Contents

"Never be afraid to dream too big.
Anything is possible if you work hard for it."

Chapter 1
Russian Roots

Valeri Liukin was a shining star on the Russian Men's Gymnastics team. By the end of 1987, the handsome, muscular athlete owned a staggering seven world and European championship medals, including five gold.

While performing on a gymnastics tour spanning Australia and New Zealand, Valeri's best friend and fellow gymnast, Evgeny Marchenko, introduced him to Anna Kotchneva. The lithe, elegant rhythmic gymnast had just scored a gold and two bronze medals at the 1987 World Championships.

Valeri fell in love instantly. Anna, however, initially showed little romantic interest in return. At a striking 5'7", the leggy knockout deemed her 5'4" suitor too short! Unaccustomed to losing, a determined Valeri relentlessly pursued his crush, and by the tour's end, he captured Anna's heart.

A year later, at the 1988 Barcelona Olympics, Valeri nabbed gold medals in the team and horizontal bar competitions. He also took home all-around and parallel bars silver medals. Despite his enormous success in Spain, Valeri felt extremely disappointed with his all-around silver medal. The young man hated losing and felt extreme frustration at having come so close to his sport's most prestigious title.

Sadly, unexpected bouts with the measles and chicken pox kept Anna from competing at the Olympics. However, the soft-spoken young woman drowned her sorrows by planning a dream wedding to the man of her dreams. Several months after the couple's honeymoon, Anna discovered she was expecting a baby! The news thrilled her more than any Olympic competition ever could. She couldn't wait to be a mother.

On October 30th 1989, in a Moscow hospital, Valeri and Anna welcomed a daughter into the world. They named their baby, Anastasia Valerivna, but they called her Nastia, for short. The smitten couple couldn't believe they were blessed with such a perfect child. With her soft blonde hair and beautiful blue eyes, the adorable infant looked as if she belonged on baby magazine covers!

A driven man with lofty ambition, Valeri wanted only the best for his young family. The new husband and father began formulating his lifelong dream of moving to the United States. He admired a country that offered endless opportunities for hard-working individuals. So in 1992, the Liukins made the courageous decision to leave behind their home country and emigrate to America.

At first, the close-knit family settled in New Orleans, Louisiana, a beautiful port city known for its jazz music, French architecture and tasty cuisine. The experienced gymnast quickly found employment as an assistant coach at a gymnastics training center where he gained valuable experience.

Valeri possessed bigger career aspirations, though. He wanted to run his own business and longed to establish a world-class training center for competitive gymnasts.

"We'd started dreaming about our own empire," he told *The Dallas Morning News*. "I started working very, very hard because I wanted to be somebody."

However, securing the necessary money for such a massive project proved a challenging task for a young immigrant with very little money. Still, Valeri felt determined to see his vision through, so he began raising the necessary cash. For starters, Valeri sold his apartment in Europe, setting aside the profit. Then he entered and won a professional gymnastics competition. The $15,000 prize money provided him with the ability to look for property on which to build his training facility.

After much debate and careful consideration, the Liukins, along with their old friend and business partner Evgeny Marchenko, moved to Plano, Texas. After scouting several potential properties, the men chose an abandoned supermarket as the site of their training center. Scrimping and saving every last penny, the best friends completed much of the building's remodeling themselves. They worked long, grueling hours patching holes, painting walls and installing flooring until they transformed the former grocery store into a respectable gym.

In 1994, they officially opened their training center: the World Olympic and Gymnastics Academy, or WOGA, for short. As new business owners, Valeri and Evgeny often spent 12-hour days at their gym as they strove to make their venture a success.

Anna helped out at the gym as much as possible. However, her main priority lay with raising her daughter who had developed into a bundle of energy. Now five years old,

Nastia attended kindergarten where she was one of the most active children in her class.

World Olympic and Gymnastics Academy
(Joseph Dzidrums)

Widely regarded as gymnastics royalty, with a top facility at their disposal, many expected Valeri and Anna to groom Nastia to follow in their footsteps. However, nothing was further from the truth. Knowing the enormous sacrifices that gymnastics required, the protective parents felt no desire to introduce their daughter to the difficult sport.

Instead Anna and Valeri enrolled Nastia in piano lessons. The young girl's teacher noticed something right away. Her student showed a strong musical talent. Except despite her natural artistic leanings, Nastia quickly grew bored with the instrument.

Meanwhile, with their business struggling to survive its infant years, Anna was needed at the gym more and more. Because the Liukins lived on a strict family budget, they could not afford the luxury of babysitters. As a result, Nastia hung out at the gym quite regularly. As each day passed, she became more and more exposed to competitive gymnastics, and it intrigued her.

The young girl's curious blue eyes grew big whenever she watched well-toned athletes training on various apparatuses. The balance beam looked scary but challenging. How exciting to witness gymnasts soaring through the air on floor and vault! It felt thrilling to see powerful athletes swing gracefully on the uneven bars! In record time, the tiny girl with pigtails fell in love with the sport.

"I want to do gymnastics, too," little Nastia begged her parents.

"Absolutely not," they replied firmly.

"Neither of my parents ever pushed me in gymnastics," Nastia later reminisced. "They kind of pushed me the opposite way when I was little. They knew how hard it was. They didn't want me to do it."

But Nastia, though a tiny girl, had her father's strong stubborn streak in her. She refused to take no for an answer.

Sometimes when her parents were busy training athletes, Nastia would run to a nearby floor mat and perform somersaults. She had talent, too! With gymnastics genes running through her, Valeri and Anna's only child showed a quick aptitude and astonishing flexibility.

Nastia wasn't just enamored with the tumbling side of the sport, though. She also loved the musical aspect of it. The young girl often quietly hummed classical music while she performed impromptu floor routines!

Finally, Valeri and Anna threw up their hands in defeat. Their daughter clearly loved gymnastics and longed to pursue her passion. Who were they to stand in the way of her dream?

"OK," they relented one fateful day. "You can take gymnastics classes."

Little Nastia squealed with delight and jumped up and down in excitement. She could hardly wait to begin her lessons.

Valeri and Anna couldn't help but smile at their daughter's enthusiasm. They loved seeing her happy. Besides, maybe she would eventually tire of the activity, as she did with piano lessons. Perhaps her love affair with the sport would be short-lived.

Little did they know at the time - Nastia's gymnastics' journey had barely begun!

Nastia at 2003 Parkettes Invitational
(Pam Mayer)

"*My parents tell me, when I was very, very young,
I used to run around with a ribbon in my hand,
throw it up in the air,
then run out and do a cartwheel.*"

Chapter 2
Little Gymnast

Nastia loved nearly everything about gymnastics. For starters, she thrived on the physical challenges the sport offered. It felt great to gain a new skill after investing so much time to learn it.

The eager gymnast soon discovered that she possessed a natural gift for the uneven bars. She loved flying through the air and swinging from one bar to the next. It became her favorite event to train.

That's not to say she didn't enjoy the other apparatuses, though. Nastia loved the exciting challenge of performing on the balance beam where equilibrium and flexibility were essential. She also adored the tumbling and dancing associated with the floor exercise. And although the youngster considered vault her hardest event, she thrived on sprinting down a runway and leaping over the horse.

The expressive young girl also adored the sport's creative side. Whenever Nastia heard the opening notes of her floor music, she assumed the precise posture of a world-class ballerina and used her entire body, right down to her fingertips, to express the piece.

Truth be told, Nastia was also a girly girl. She adored dressing up in feminine gymnastics leotards with matching hair bands. She especially loved wearing pink since that was her favorite color.

"I never wanted to take my leotard off," Nastia later told *USA Today.* "I wanted to sleep in it all the time. They would try to come in when I was asleep and take it off. If I woke up, I was hysterically crying because I wanted to keep it on."

Nastia practiced at her parents' gym nearly every day. Blessed with natural talent and a voracious desire to learn, the youngster picked up difficult skills at lightning speed. She soon eclipsed gymnasts much older than her.

When Nastia turned six years old, she entered her first competition. Representing WOGA, she competed against girls from a nearby gym. The precocious youth flourished under the spotlight and fell in love with competing. She especially delighted in the awards ceremony following the event, where organizers presented her with a bright ribbon and a shiny medal!

Much to some people's surprise, Valeri did not initially coach his daughter. A young gym owner working to keep his new business afloat, he often worked taxing hours and did not have the luxury of working with Nastia a lot. As a result, the burgeoning gymnast received lessons from her mom or other gym workers.

Whenever the Liukins left the gym and returned home to their modest apartment, they cherished family time. Mom and daughter often cuddled up together on their couch and watched *Sesame Street*. The educational *PBS* children's show proved quite useful, as it taught Nastia her alphabet and helped Anna strengthen her English skills!

Still deeply tied to their heritage, the Liukins returned to Russia at least once a year. Nastia loved visiting extended family and seeing where her parents had lived for most of their life. The articulate youth often spoke to her grandparents in Russian. In fact, she could speak her parents' native language just as well as English!

In the summer of 1996, six-year-old Nastia spent several days glued to the television set watching the Atlanta Olympics. Needless to say, she soaked up the gymnastics' coverage and cheered for the Americans who, buoyed by Keri Strug's heroic vault, won the team gold in history-making fashion.

However, Nastia most admired Ukraine's Lilia Podkopayeva who won the all-around competition. Considered the sport's most esteemed title, the all-around crowns the gymnast who receives the highest combined score in all

Young Nastia
(Pam Mayer)

four apparatuses. Nastia loved watching the balletic gymnast perform in every event. Lilia represented the complete package. She boasted strong technical skills with breathtaking artistry. The youngest Liukin dreamed of someday becoming an exquisite artist and strong technician, just like her hero.

In early 2000, WOGA became the training home of Vanessa Atler, a high-profile Olympic hopeful for the Sydney

Games. On one occasion, the legendary Bela Karolyi, former coach of gymnastics legends Nadia Comaneci and Mary Lou Retton, visited the gym to assess her physical fitness. Instead of focusing on Vanessa, though, he watched ten-year-old Nastia with great interest!

"Her personality commanded attention," he told *Newsweek*. "She had this total confidence."

At this point, Nastia competed in local competitions quite regularly, winning many of them. She delighted in performing for audiences and judges. Nothing thrilled her more than executing a new skill under the pressure of competition. Before long, medals, trophies and ribbons cluttered her bedroom shelves.

One day at the gym, while spotting her on the uneven bars, Nastia's instructor accidentally elbowed her in the face. The young girl wound up sporting a black eye. A very protective father, Valeri decided then and there that he would take over his daughter's coaching.

"From that day, I said, 'No more,'" he told *USA Today*. "I was really scared for her, always. That's the only reason I started coaching her."

Nastia felt delighted with her new coaching situation. She had watched old videotapes of her father's competitive days and looked up to him as a gymnast. She eagerly anticipated spending extra time with her dad and vowed to work very hard to please him.

Together, the duo would make huge waves in the gymnastics world.

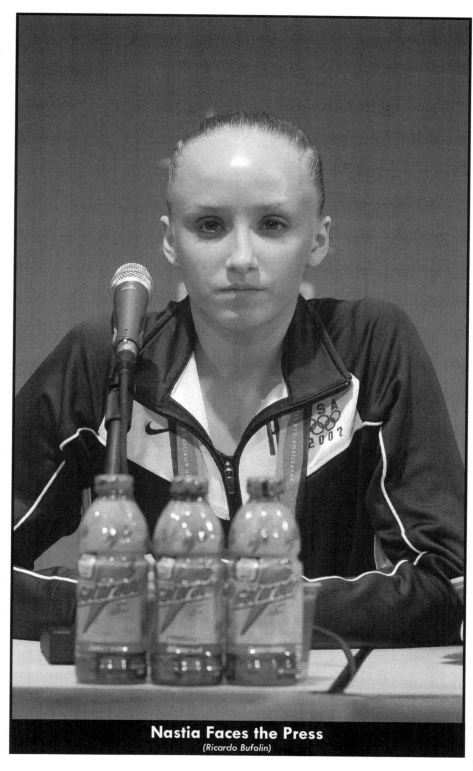

Nastia Faces the Press
(Ricardo Bufolin)

"Exercise is extremely important for young kids –
or any age. It's good for your health.
It's good for your heart. It's good for everything."

Chapter 3
A Competitor is Born

In a typical competition, a female gymnast ideally has the opportunity to win six medals. First up, gymnasts may compete in the team competition. The all-around event usually follows. Finally, in event finals, medals are awarded to the top three scorers in each apparatus.

Gymnastics features ten different levels with level one as the simplest and ten as the most advanced. Once an athlete reaches elite status, they become eligible to represent their country at the Olympics, world championships and other international competitions.

Now a seasoned competitor, Nastia advanced swiftly up the levels. Among her early highlights, she delighted in winning the Level 6 State Championships and felt equally proud to qualify for the Level 9 Western National Championships.

By January of 2002, twelve-year-old Nastia competed on the junior international level. She made her elite debut at the WOGA Classic. Unfortunately, the young gymnast nursed a bad back and fell on all four apparatuses. She finished sixth among eight competitors.

Meanwhile, Nastia's good friend, Carly Patterson, won the junior event. The chatty teenager from Louisiana, coached by Evgeny Marchenko, garnered much attention in the gymnastics' world. She boasted difficult skills with explosive gymnastics. With the 2004 Athens Games just two years away, many felt Carly represented America's best chance to win the esteemed Olympic all-around title.

Only a year apart in age, Nastia and Carly were good friends. They spent much time together in the gym and even socialized outside of WOGA, too. The two often hung out at the local mall where they'd catch a movie or shop for the latest fashions.

That summer Nastia flew to Cleveland, Ohio, to compete at the 2002 U.S. Gymnastics Championships. She hoped to finish high enough to secure a spot on the national team which would make her eligible to compete internationally. Her dream seemed in jeopardy, though, during the all-around competition when she fell on the uneven bars, injured her arm and could not finish her routine.

Valeri cast a worried look at Nastia. Concerned for her safety, he felt uncertain whether she should continue competing.

"Do you want to withdraw from the competition?" he asked.

"No," Nastia replied firmly. "I want to finish the event."

The strong competitor quickly refocused and performed strongly on the remaining apparatuses. When the championships ended, she scanned the scoreboard anxiously and smiled with relief at her 15th place finish. By the skin of her teeth, the twelve-year-old had grabbed a spot on the national team.

"It's been my dream since I was little," a gleeful Nastia told *International Gymnast Magazine*.

Following the U.S. Championships, Nastia attended a training camp run by Bela Karolyi and his wife, Marta, USA Gymnastics' national team coordinator. Surrounded by the Sam Houston National Forest in Texas, the camp regularly hosted the country's best gymnasts for training sessions and mock competitions. An invitation to the camp indicated that you were one of gymnastics' brightest stars and would be seriously considered for international competitions.

Nastia arrived at Bela and Marta's 1,200-acre ranch with high hopes of winning an international assignment. The enormous facility featured a 3,500 square-foot gymnasium complex, a lake, petting zoo, an Olympic-size swimming pool, tennis courts and more.

Nastia stayed in a cabin with several other top gymnasts. She quickly became friends with the other girls and enjoyed the strong camaraderie the camp built. More importantly, Nastia excelled in the training sessions and meets. By the time the teenager returned home, she felt confident that she had left a good impression on Marta.

Her instincts proved correct when USA Gymnastics selected Nastia to represent the United States at the Junior Pan American Games in Santo Domingo, Dominican Republic. Though inexperienced on the international level, the focused gymnast appeared fearless on the world stage. Nastia's strong routines helped the U.S. win the team title. Then she claimed individual silver medals in the all-around, balance beam and floor exercise events.

In just a few months, the tiny Texan quickly established herself as a rising star in gymnastics. Look out, world!

Nastia Liukin Homecoming Parade
(Christopher Longoria)

By the time Nastia celebrated her thirteenth birthday, she was considered one of America's top gymnasts. At the USA/Japan Dual in Houston, Texas, the rising star won gold medals in the team competition, all-around, uneven bars, balance beam and floor exercise.

Despite her impressive new stature, though, Nastia remained your typical All-American girl. She attended Spring Creek Academy, a private college prep school in Plano, Texas, and counted math as her favorite subject. The ambitious teenager even entertained thoughts of becoming a marine biologist.

In her spare time, Nastia enjoyed physical activities, like snow skiing and swimming. Of course, she liked spending quiet, relaxing days at home, too. She sometimes lounged around the house chatting on the Internet or watching television. Her favorite TV shows? *Boy Meets World*, *Lizzie Maguire*, *Even Stevens* and *So Little Time*.

By the time the 2003 U.S. Gymnastics Championships arrived, most regarded Nastia as the heavy favorite to claim the junior all-around title. Upon arriving in Milwaukee, Wisconsin, the focused competitor took her front-runner status seriously, wanting to confirm her reputation as America's top junior gymnast.

In the end, Nastia handily won her first U.S. championship, winning four gold medals overall. She claimed first place in the all-around, uneven bars, balance beam and floor exercise.

"It was really exciting," Nastia smiled. "It's really cool standing up on the podium."

"This is her Olympic Games," Valeri told *The Dallas Morning News*. "This is her day. I'm very proud, as a coach and a dad."

"She is a special talent," an impressed Marta Karolyi commented. "She has big promise for 2008."

In early August of that same year, Nastia competed at the 2003 Pan American Games. Wearing a fiery red, white and blue leotard, the agile teen contributed greatly to the United States' team gold. She then finished second, behind teammate Chellsie Memmel, in the all-around competition. The soaring gymnast rounded out the competition with a gold medal on the balance beam and third place finishes in the uneven bars and floor exercise.

"We all had a good meet and we all did great as a team, trying to help each other," a modest Nastia said.

"She went out there 11 times and hit all 11 routines," Valeri told *The Dallas Morning News*. "As a coach, that is what you dream about. You can't do any better than that."

"She's stepped up to a different level, both mentally and physically," he continued. "She's now a solid international gymnast. She's proved she can take on any kind of competition."

Shortly after winning the Pan Am Games, the ladies gymnastics team received a phone call from George W. Bush, President of the United States! An excited Nastia started to introduce herself to him, when he interrupted her.

"You're my girl from Texas," he exclaimed!

"That was really cool," an excited Nastia told the *Associated Press*. "We were very nervous at first, but that was exciting."

Later that year, producers of the *T.J. Maxx Tour of Gymnastics Champions* invited Nastia to perform in their Dallas stop at American Airlines Center. The young gymnast felt thrilled to be included in such a prestigious event and unveiled a new floor routine for the occasion. Because it was a show, spotlights were used in lieu of floor lighting. It was quite a challenge for Nastia to complete her tumbling passes because her landings were blind! Nevertheless, she executed a strong routine and felt honored to join a strong cast that also included world champions Carly Patterson, Chellsie Memmel and Hollie Vise.

The following season marked the year of the Summer Olympics. The world's best athletes would converge in Athens, Greece, to compete in various sporting events, including gymnastics, with dreams of winning a medal for their country.

Although many regarded Nastia as one of America's top gymnasts, she could not compete at the 2004 Olympics. The International Gymnastics Federation, the sport's official governing body, required that gymnasts be at least 16, or turn 16 within the calendar year, to compete in senior-level events.

Ten months too young to compete in Athens, Nastia remained at the junior level for another season. She instead arrived in Nashville, Tennessee, poised to win a second national junior title. The gymnast performed her programs effortlessly and easily won her second straight all-around gold medal. In fact, her impressive scores would have placed her third in the senior ladies competition, and her balance beam score was higher than any senior woman's score!

Nastia's ineligibility to compete in the 2004 Olympics saddened many gymnastics fans and insiders. Marta Karolyi, the woman almost solely responsible for selecting America's gymnastics team, expressed frustration with the rule. She even stated that Nastia would have made the women's team if she had been age-eligible!

Meanwhile, Carly Patterson, Nastia's close friend and training mate, entered the Athens Games as the top American gymnast. Coming off a team gold and an all-around silver medal at the 2003 World Championships, the bubbly teen saw her image plastered on McDonald's cups and bags. She also enjoyed an endorsement deal with Visa. Meanwhile, various news organizations showed up at WOGA to chat with the Athens-bound athlete. Because Nastia was so close to Carly, it almost felt like she was experiencing the Olympics buildup herself!

Then as fate would have it, Nastia ended up playing a prominent role in the Athens Games after all. Adidas, a sports apparel company, asked the gymnast to star in a commercial that played heavily throughout the games' broadcast. In the ad, Nastia recreated Nadia Comaneci's famous 1976 uneven bars program while clever editors combined footage of the gymnastics legend's original performance. As a result, Nastia and Nadia appeared to be performing the routine together! This clever commercial added much buzz to Nastia's image.

In the meantime, Carly enjoyed a highly successful Athens experience, becoming the first American to win the women's all-around competition in a fully attended Olympics. She also took silver medals in team and balance beam events.

Nastia was in her Algebra II class when Karen Morrell, the director of the school for WOGA gymnasts and other elite athletes, summoned her out of class to deliver the news that Carly had won the all-around title. Excited for her friend, Nastia squealed with delight at the news.

"It was an incredible moment," Karen told *The Dallas Morning News.* "Here I was delivering the news of one Olympic gold medal to the girl who may very well win the next one."

Later that evening, Nastia, Hollie Vise and over a hundred other Carly supporters gathered at Austin Avenue Grill to watch their friend make history. As they sat at tables while glued to the restaurant's big screen televisions, Nastia felt thrilled for her friend. She couldn't help wondering if one day she might compete at the Olympics herself.

"Now that you see your best friend winning the Olympic gold, that just motivates you even more," a determined Nastia said.

Proud of their golden girl, WOGA hung a huge banner on the wall of their gym, congratulating Carly on her historic accomplishments. Every day when Nastia walked into the gym, the large sign greeted her. Every day the hard-working teenager felt more motivated than ever to make her own Olympic dreams come true.

"*Gymnastics is such a technical sport.
You use your body for everything.*"

Chapter 4
Senior Level

Indianapolis, Indiana's state capital, hosted the 2005 U.S. Gymnastics Championships. Nastia would finally compete at the senior level. Chellsie Memmel, a two-time world champion, was expected to challenge her for the all-around title.

Nastia arrived at the 18,000+ seat Conseco Fieldhouse for day one of the all-around competition. The strong favorite wore a white leotard with her blonde hair swept into a dainty ponytail.

Nastia began the competition with a strong vault. On her second apparatus, she executed a beautiful uneven bars routine. Halfway through the first day of nationals, Nastia looked poised to win her first senior title. Then she hit a roadblock.

Throughout the beam, normally one of her best events, Nastia seemed shaky with several balance checks. Then on her dismount, she landed short and nearly fell to the floor.

"It was just one of those fluke mistakes," Nastia later remarked.

Sure enough, Nastia bounced back with a strong floor routine. Nevertheless, by the end of night one, the normally solid gymnast found herself in third place behind Chellsie and a powerful gymnast named Jana Bieger.

Nastia Signs Autographs

Backstage in the media zone, reporters questioned Nastia about her surprise third place standing. The levelheaded athlete responded with the maturity of a veteran competitor.

"Of course, I want to win, but you're not always going to win every competition," she stressed. "Seniors is a lot different. There are a lot more competitors, and it's harder. I know for a fact that I'm not always going to be on the top."

When asked how she would approach the second day of all-around competition, Nastia appeared focused and ready to meet the challenge.

"Things are going to happen…just like they did tonight," she stressed. "So I've just got to go in and work a little extra and I'll be good."

On the evening of August 13th, Nastia walked into the arena wearing a striking white and fluorescent green leotard. She appeared cool, collected and ready to compete.

The steady gymnast began the competition on her best event, the uneven bars. She unveiled a performance nothing short of breathtaking.

"Exquisite," raved *NBC* commentator Elfi Schlegel. "She works the uneven bars with such perfect form and amplitude."

Afterwards, Nastia traveled to the balance beam, scene of her day one mishap. This time, however, she felt determined to conquer the apparatus.

"Here's where you'll get to see trademark Nastia Liukin," Olympic champion Tim Daggett remarked. "Beautiful long lines and perfect form."

Nastia Prepares for Beam
(Ricardo Bufolin)

Nastia was remarkable throughout the apparatus. When she landed her dismount, the crowd erupted into huge applause.

Next she turned her attention to the floor exercise. This challenging event allowed her to showcase her elegant form, amazing flexibility and phenomenal dance skills. She turned in a superb performance.

As she stood on the runway and faced her final apparatus, the vault, the all-around title lay within Nastia's grasp. She took a deep breath and visualized herself executing a perfect 1½ Yurchenko.

It worked! Nastia landed a great vault. She smiled with relief and joy as she jogged off the floor and into her dad's loving arms. Daughter and father shared a long hug and celebrated

Nastia: Gymnastics' Supergirl
(Jeffrey Poulter)

her fine performance. Waiting in the wings, best friend Carly Patterson, who was watching the event as a spectator, embraced her former training mate.

When Nastia's 9.483 score was posted, she was officially the winner. The young girl from Plano, Texas, had become America's new national champion!

"I didn't really think about trying to get first place," Nastia later remarked. "I just tried to focus on doing my routines like I do in practice. I was just trying to hit four for four tonight."

"Nationals is a two day competition," she continued. "After the first day if you have a little mistake, you can never give up. Even when you feel like it's all over, it's never over, so just keep fighting your way through it."

"I'm proud of her as a father and a coach," Valeri told the *Associated Press*. "You can only dream of your baby working hard to get where she wants to be. And as a coach, what can I say? Look at the results."

"I don't do gymnastics for the medals.
I love to compete."

Chapter 5
The Same Nastia

Now the queen of USA Gymnastics, Nastia commanded much media focus throughout the sports world. In fact, she received attention elsewhere, too. A week after her nationals' victory, Nastia celebrated her big win by attending an Avril Lavigne concert with Carly. To their surprise, people recognized them and asked for their autographs!

Of course, the gymnastics world also seemed enamored with Nastia. Her gymnastics pedigree, the daughter of two world champions, intrigued many. Not to mention, her beautiful line, astonishing flexibility and unparalleled artistry set her miles apart from her contemporaries.

Though the Olympics were four years away, people already called her the favorite for the all-around title at the 2008 Beijing Games. After all, WOGA had produced one Olympic champion in Carly. Was Nastia next in line?

"Every single day I walk in and the sign is on the door: golden girl," Nastia remarked. "The big Wheaties box with her on it. All the posters in the gym - Olympic gold medalist Carly Patterson. She leaves the country as just the national champion and comes back as the world's hero."

"It just makes it so much more realistic when you see Carly came up through the gym," Valeri commented. "It's great for Nastia. She can really believe that it's possible."

Nastia on the Red Carpet
(Jamie Lantzy)

"You see how hard she trains, what she had to do, what she had to go through," Nastia agreed. "So you know what it takes to be Olympic champion."

Despite all the fanfare his daughter received, Valeri remained a proud but protective father, first and foremost. He worried that expectations might be set too high for the young gymnast.

"Lately people talk about her a little too much," Valeri said apprehensively. "She does get a lot of attention right now. She's just a gymnast and that's how we take it."

"It's going to be hard when she's not going to win," he continued realistically. "It will happen for sure. She's just a human and she will make a mistake, and I think this is going to be hard for her. It's going to happen sooner or later with everybody. We're not machines; we're human."

Indeed Nastia was human. In fact, she was your typical teenager girl. When she wasn't attending school or training at the gym, you could find her at home. Some of the time she spent clowning around on the computer, instant messaging with her close friends. Other times she liked to cuddle up in a comfortable spot and become absorbed in a good novel while her dog, Lexi, lay by her side. Her favorite books? She read *Twilight* and *A-List*, a popular series about a group of friends from Beverly Hills.

Nastia also enjoyed watching other sports. She never missed the Tour de France and considered Lance Armstrong her favorite cyclist. The well-rounded sports fan cheered for NBA's Dallas Mavericks. She also watched figure skating and cited Sasha Cohen as her favorite athlete in that sport.

When Nastia was in the mood for a movie, she got comfy and watched something from her DVD collection. In particular, comedies were her cup of tea. She especially liked the movies: *Napoleon Dynamite, Mean Girls* and *Legally Blonde.*

Being a very musical performer, Nastia loved all kinds of music. Her favorite artists were Kelly Clarkson and Ashlee Simpson, while she counted Fall Out Boy, My Chemical Romance, Green Day and Click Five as groups she enjoyed. She also liked Carly Patterson's new single. Yes, the Olympic champion had begun pursuing a recording career!

Still, at the end of the day, gymnastics owned Nastia's heart. One could catch her at the gym training 36 hours a week, every day of the week but Sunday. The whole while she kept her eye on the Beijing Olympics.

"Everything seems like it just keeps going really fast," she remarked "I think these last few years leading up to the Olympics…I think they'll go by really fast."

With each passing day, Nastia became a bigger celebrity. Despite her newfound stardom, the grounded teenager insisted that she had not changed one bit.

"With both of my parents being successful gymnasts, and Carly training here, I guess I can see where people say I could be the next big thing, but I try not to take in too much of that," she mused. "I don't feel like I'm the next best thing. I feel like I'm the same Nastia."

Nastia Rocks the Pink

"You have to be determined,
and you have to be in the gym every day,
and you have to get through the hard days.
Anybody can train on the easy days,
but if you can get through the hard days,
when you don't feel good, and just work and work,
that's when it pays off."

Chapter 6
2005 World Championships

In late November, Nastia flew to Melbourne, Australia, to compete at the 2005 World Gymnastics Championships. She hoped to leave the historic city with her first world medal.

The top 24 girls comprised the all-around competition. Nastia and Chellsie Memmel, representing the American girls, would also be each other's biggest competition.

Wearing a gorgeous red leotard with sheer sleeves, Nastia began the competition on the vault, where she took a hop on her landing. Then she hit a beautiful bars routine with a perfect stuck landing on the dismount. A steady balance beam worker, she unveiled a strong program that showcased her terrific flexibility and impressive amplitude. With one event remaining, Nastia stood in first place with Chellsie close behind in second.

Defying enormous pressure, Nastia performed a strong floor exercise routine. Her mature dance skills and superb flexibility stood out from the pack. Chellsie, on the other hand, relied on her enormous power and high skills to also garner a huge score. When the competition ended, Chellsie posted a total score of 37.824, while Nastia netted a 37.823. By 1/1000 of a point, Chellsie became world all-around champion.

Naturally, Nastia initially felt quite disappointed with the result. She had come so close to winning the top prize at her first world championships. As the moments passed, however,

Nastia Models Vanilla Star Jeans

she appreciated the enormity of her achievement. At her first worlds, she won a silver medal in the all-around, a feat most gymnasts would never accomplish! Soon enough, she embraced her second place finish.

"(Winning the silver medal) feels great," Nastia smiled. "I've been working really hard for this so it's great to get the silver medal. To get a reward for all the training I have done, that's really good."

Nastia still had the opportunity to win three more world medals. In the event finals, she qualified in floor, balance beam and uneven bars. A strong competitor, she vowed to perform assertively in her remaining events.

Wearing a pretty red and white leotard, Nastia was favored to take a medal in the uneven bars. She swung effortlessly from bar to bar with the grace and precise line of a world-class ballerina.

"Nastia's body lines, her long arms and long legs make her bars look that much more pretty," praised Tasha Schwikert, a former two-time U.S. champion.

"This is more aggressive than I've seen her in the past," raved Olympic champion Bart Conner.

At the end of the uneven bars final, Nastia stood in first place. She had done it! She won the gold medal! Meanwhile, Chellsie took silver and Great Britain's Beth Tweddle won the bronze.

"I feel great. I know I did a good routine. I knew I could pull it off," Nastia said happily. "After that it was just up to the judges."

Nastia wasn't done winning gold medals, however. The next day she entered the Rod Laver Arena with dreams of winning more hardware. On the daunting balance beam, she gave another tour de force performance to take first place ahead of Chellsie and third place finisher Catalina Ponor of Romania.

Then on the floor exercise, Nastia gave another sterling performance. This time she took the silver medal behind teammate Alicia Sacramone. All in all, Nastia left Australia with two gold and two silver medals. Not too shabby for a rookie!

"I can't find any other word, it was just very spectacular," Valeri told the *Associated Press*. "It's amazing."

"The whole experience has been great," Nastia remarked. "Four medals at a world championships myself, there is nothing else I can ask for."

"Even though gymnastics is a hard sport, you always have to make sure you're having fun, and you're loving what you're doing because you spend so many hours in the gym. And always give 100% and try your hardest every time."

Chapter 7
Movie Star & Setbacks

Nastia Liukin - World Champion. Nastia Liukin - U.S Champion. Nastia Liukin - Movie Star?

In April of 2006, *Stick It!*, a motion picture centered around elite gymnastics premiered in movie theaters across the country. The story focused on a juvenile delinquent/ex-gymnast, played by Missy Peregrym, who returns to gymnastics and shakes things up in the conservative sport. One of her competitors? None other than Nastia Liukin!

Nastia spent several days on the set of the movie filming scenes as she played herself competing at the U.S. Championships. Of course, the teenager felt thrilled to be part of such a major production.

"The set of *Stick It!* was awesome!" Nastia wrote on her official website, *NastiaLiukin.com*. "Everybody was so nice and positive! Acting was sooo much fun and I hope to do more of it soon!!"

The film's actors were equally thrilled to work with world-class athletes. In fact, they looked to the gymnasts for help with their characters.

"We were all so fortunate to have with us in our company two world class gymnasts, Isabelle Severino and Nastia Liukin," Academy Award winner Jeff Bridges remarked. "Both girls helped the actresses immensely, but also I would go to them all the time and say 'How would your coach behave at this particular time?' and they would always have a very quick answer for me. They inspired our actresses and our actresses inspired them."

Stick It!
(Touchstone Pictures)

When Nastia wasn't acting in feature films and competing as a world-class athlete, she devoted time to her schooling. With the SATs quickly approaching, she spent many hours studying for the important college entrance exams. The hardworking teen hoped to attend Southern Methodist University the next year and perhaps eventually transfer to Brown University, an Ivy League school in Rhode Island.

Meanwhile, Nastia's gymnastics continued to flourish. She opened the season with all-around victories at the 2006 American Cup and the Pacific Alliance Championships.

In August she traveled to St. Paul, Minnesota, to defend her title at the 2006 U.S. Gymnastics Championships. Wearing a white leotard with blue trim, Nastia gave some truly breathtaking performances, particularly on balance beam and uneven bars.

"These lines that you're seeing from Nastia come from her mom, Anna, who was actually a world-class rhythmic gymnast," Elfi Schlegel raved. "What she does in between all the acrobatic skills is so difficult, I can't even tell you. The pointing of the feet... The stretched legs... Very hard dance."

As usual, Nastia racked up a huge score on her best event, the uneven bars. No one in the world could swing on the apparatus as well as the Plano native.

"She's world champion on this event and deserves to be," Tim Daggett remarked.

At the end of the competition, Nastia successfully defended her all-around title! All in all, she had won four straight national championships, two on the junior level and two on the senior level.

"It feels awesome to win," Nastia smiled modestly after the competition.

One of Nastia's biggest fans? None other than Marta Karolyi – not an easy woman to please.

"She has almost perfect technical execution," the national team coordinator raved. "From the moment she broke on the international scene, she was recognized as one of the top competitors."

Not surprisingly, Nastia was selected to compete at the world championships in Aarhus, Denmark. After coming so close the previous year, she hoped to win the all-around title.

Unfortunately, a few weeks after nationals, Nastia experienced an injury that destroyed her world all-around chances and nearly derailed her career altogether. At a training camp, she sprained her ankle while practicing a floor routine. Her foot immediately swelled up like a balloon. Little did the gymnast know at the time, she had also sustained ligament damage.

Nastia iced her injury and underwent acupuncture and bone stimulation in order to speed up her recovery. However, in the end, the unexpected injury prevented her from competing in the all-around at worlds. In fact, doctors limited her participation to uneven bars only.

"It's a little disappointing, especially coming off nationals, where I did so well," Nastia told the *Associated Press*. "But you kind of have to deal with what happens."

"We selected her to the team because we expect her to be there for at least one event," Marta Karolyi told *The Dallas Morning News*. "That's very important for the team result."

Despite competing in only one event at worlds, Nastia netted the highest individual score, 16.2, of any woman competitor in any discipline. Her huge score contributed greatly to the American women winning the silver medal in the team event. Meanwhile, the Chinese women won their first ever team title.

"It's always a great accomplishment to win any medal," Nastia commented. "We are a little disappointed but very proud of one another."

A few days later, Nastia added another silver medal to her collection when she finished second in the bars final. Had

Subway Commercial

she not taken a small hop on the landing of her dismount, she likely would have taken the gold.

When Nastia returned home, her friends threw her a surprise birthday party. Now seventeen years old, she owned a driver's license, so her parents presented her with a BMW Z4! A few weeks later, Nastia's birthday month was doubly special when her grandparents flew in from Moscow for a visit.

In late fall, Nastia underwent surgery on her ankle to remove several bone chips. Afterwards, she embarked on painful rehabilitation. Despite the setbacks, the willful teenager felt determined to overcome any physical or mental roadblocks on the way to recovery.

"I never think, 'What if I roll my ankle again?'" she told *Newsweek*. "I think what it would be like to stand on top of the podium and listen to the national anthem."

*"My Dad is my biggest supporter,
and he's an inspiration to me."*

Chapter 8
Rebounding

While attempting to rebound from a serious injury, it helps if an athlete has a caring, trusting coach by his or her side. It helps even more if that coach is also your father.

One of the key ingredients to Nastia and Valeri's working relationship? Gymnastics never ruled their life. More importantly, both took care to draw a strict line between the gym and home life.

"When we get home, he's my dad," Nastia explained. "We never really talk about gym at home. Sometimes we'll watch one of my competitions but it's never every day. We just keep the gym at the gym. At home, he's just my dad."

In fact, the Liukins spent their weekends like any normal family. On some Saturdays, they lounged at the beach and barbequed or played a friendly volleyball game. Sometimes the threesome enjoyed a nice family dinner at a local restaurant. In particular, Nastia loved when they went out to eat her favorite food, sushi.

In the gym, though, Nastia and Valeri kept things strictly business-like. The headstrong teenager trusted her coach 100%. She believed he guided her toward being the best gymnast possible.

"He might be tougher on me, but I think that's good because he knows my goals," Nastia explained. "I want to be on top of the world in gymnastics so it takes toughness. It is hard some days, but that's what makes you a good gymnast."

"I think having my dad being able to catch all those tiny, tiny mistakes is really what helps me be the gymnast that I am today," she continued. "The judges are looking for all those little mistakes too, and they can spot them. My dad can spot even the tiniest details."

Though Nastia and her father proved a winning combination, Valeri also prepared his daughter for the sport's mental struggles. A former competitor himself, he stressed that competing wasn't just about winning. It was also about the journey.

"A lot of time you lose," he said. "You lose sometimes; you win a lot. This is what it takes to be a great gymnast. I know that. I've seen that. I've done that."

Nevertheless, a competitor likes to win. Valeri knew that Nastia was no exception to that rule. As competitive athletes, they shared similar mindsets.

"She reminds me of myself. I just hated second place. It was the worst for me," Valeri recalled. "There was one place for me - first. I can see that a lot in Nastia, too. That little fragile body...there's an animal inside that body."

It's a difficult task for any parent to bring up a child. It's even harder to juggle the demands of raising your daughter while also grooming her to be a top athlete. Yet, Anna Liukin best summed up the family's thoughts in a revealing television interview with *NBC*.

"Of course medals are great and it's a real pleasure to see a smile on your child's face, but it's not the most important thing in life," she stressed. "I want my daughter to be a good person. I'm just as happy when she does well at school or if she overcomes a difficult situation that life throws at you."

Nastia and her Father
(Caroline Martin)

"Gymnastics has been such a huge part of my life, and I think it always will be."

Chapter 9
2007 Season

2006 had been a difficult year for Nastia, mentally and physically. When she finally returned to competition in 2007, she did so slowly, so as not to aggravate her ankle. Instead of competing as an all-arounder, she temporarily limited herself to the role of event specialist. In early season meets, she competed on bars and beam only because neither event required running.

Meanwhile, as Nastia sat on the sidelines during major competitions, a spunky teenager from Des Moines, Iowa, burst onto the international scene. Shawn Johnson arrived on the senior level with a reputation as a strong, steady competitor with dynamic gymnastics.

Not intimidated by her new senior status, Shawn won the 2007 Tyson American Cup to great fanfare. Blessed with good looks and a sparkling smile, the bubbly teen loved to perform for crowds, and it showed in her popular gymnastics. Audiences loved the effervescent teen, and companies showered her with endorsement offers. Suddenly, media attention shifted from Nastia to USA's newest bright star.

Valeri, however, found a positive spin to Shawn's new-found celebrity. He strongly believed that Nastia's new rival would only fuel his daughter's competitive nature and strong work ethic.

"The more we have competition, the better we become as a country," he insisted.

Nastia at the 2007 Pan Am Games
(Ricardo Bufolin)

In mid-July, Nastia and her American teammates arrived in beautiful Rio de Janiero, Brazil, to compete in the Pan American Games. Thanks to outstanding efforts by all team members, the American women took home the team gold medal. In fact, they won by nearly seven whopping points over their nearest competitor, Brazil.

Although Nastia did not compete in the all-around, she qualified for two event finals. On the balance beam, she posted a 15.900 to take second place. Later on the uneven bars, she won another silver medal. Had Nastia not had an uncharacteristic fall on her dismount, she would have taken her second gold medal. All in all, she left the competition with three medals!

Nastia resumed competing on all four apparatuses at the 2007 U.S. Gymnastics Championships in San Jose, California. Appearing before a large crowd at the HP Pavilion, the world champion's flashy red and white leotard seemed appropriate attire for a star returning to the all-around competition.

Nastia began her comeback on the unforgiving balance beam. Despite a shaky dismount, the remarkable competitor delivered a strong, beautiful routine that left the *NBC* commentators uttering superlatives.

"She is an amazing athlete," Tim Daggett raved. "All over the world, the gymnastics' experts marvel at everything that she does. The body line, the precision that she works… If she's healthy, look out!"

"Everything she does, it's beautiful," Elfi Schlegel agreed. "It's clean. It's precise. She has incredible artistry."

Team USA is Golden!
(Ricardo Bufolin)

The crowd burst into hearty applause when Nastia completed her comeback performance. Familiar with her long road back from injury, they admired, not just her exquisite gymnastics, but her determination and hard work.

Without missing a beat, Nastia marched to the floor exercise next. The steely teenager delivered another great performance, earning the night's loudest applause.

Although her vault and uneven bars performances weren't up to her usual high level of excellence, Nastia felt relieved and happy when the first night ended. She sat in fifth place. Not bad for someone who hadn't competed in an all-around competition in nearly a full year!

"I forgot what it felt like to do it all," she grinned.

On day two of the all-around, Nastia debuted a more mature look with a black leotard and elegant ponytail. It seemed the little girl had grown up in the past year.

Although Nastia struggled on the floor exercise and vault, she gave exceptional performances on the beam and bars. In particular, she soared through the air with amazing height on the release moves of the latter apparatus, drawing gasps from the crowd.

For her efforts, Nastia moved up two spots in the standing to a bronze medal finish in the all-around. Shawn won her first U.S. title, while Orlando's Shayla Worley finished second.

In September, Nastia arrived in Stuttgart, Germany, for her third world championships' appearance. She was pleased to share a room with her good friend, Alicia Sacramone, a stellar vaulter and floor exercise worker from the Boston area. The two girls quickly learned, though, that they couldn't be anymore different. For starters, Nastia went to sleep early every night, while Alicia was a night owl. Then in the morning, the cheery Texan would awaken in a great mood while her roommate lay in bed grumbling with her blankets over her head! Nevertheless, the friends laughed at their differences and soon adjusted to the other person's different personality type. Nastia even began staying up later to accommodate her friend, while Alicia tried to have a more cheerful attitude in the morning.

The world championships began with the team event. Of course, Nastia, Shawn and Alicia were USA's biggest stars.

The Americans Flash Their Hardware
(Ricardo Bufolin)

However, they were joined by some very strong teammates: Samantha Peszek, Ivana Hong and Shayla Worley.

On day one of competition, the American girls grabbed a commanding lead of nearly four points. Notably, Nastia gave one of her finest bars performances ever. When she finished an ecstatic U.S. contingent embraced her. Valeri and Marta Karolyi offered bear hugs, while her teammates gave her enthusiastic high fives.

The American girls ran into slight trouble on the final day of competition, however. Nastia and Shawn both counted falls on the balance beam. Yet, on the final apparatus of the night, the U.S. team delivered strong floor exercise routines to rally back to first place.

Nastia and her teammates won America's first team gold medal in four years. In fact, they became the first U.S. squad to win a world championship on foreign soil. Delighted with their history-making victory, the girls gathered for an emotional group hug in a jubilant celebration.

Nastia Flips for the Beam
(Getty Images)

"We all started crying," Nastia remarked afterwards. "It's such a great feeling to know that finally we're on top of the world again."

A few days later, Nastia competed in her first world all-around competition in two years. Wearing a sparkling blue leotard, she began the competition with the vault and completed a strong Yurchenko 1½. Pleased with her effort, she flashed a huge smile on the landing.

Nastia moved to her best event next, the uneven bars. Armed with the most difficult routine in the competition, she performed it beautifully and moved into first place in the standings.

"What a tough young lady she is, coming back from a severe ankle injury that has plagued her all this year," Olympic champion Bart Conner remarked.

Balance beam marked Nastia's third apparatus of the night. After a strong start, she suffered a devastating fall on a tumbling pass. Just like that, her all-around medal chances disintegrated. A tough competitor to the end, the gutsy teen continued to attack her program.

"She's so aggressive, even after a fall," Bart praised. "Right when some athletes appear to give up, she just appears to get tougher. That's the kind of quality you like to see in a gymnast."

Nastia finished the night in fifth place. Despite the overwhelming disappointment she felt over missing out on an all-around title, the lithe teenager kept her composure, displaying a remarkably strong sportsmanship.

Nastia Listens to the National Anthem
(Ricardo Bufolin)

"It's a little disappointing just knowing that, if I didn't have that mistake, I was probably able to place in the top three," she admitted through tears. "So I'm replaying that over in my mind."

Meanwhile, Shawn snatched the all-around gold, becoming just the fourth American woman to win the title. Nastia lavished only compliments on her young teammate.

"I'm really excited for Shawn," she said. "It's great to see someone like that. It's great to know she's on your team, especially with the Olympics coming up."

All hope for another individual world gold medal was not lost, however. Nastia qualified for the uneven bars and balance beam finals. On the former event, she narrowly lost the gold to

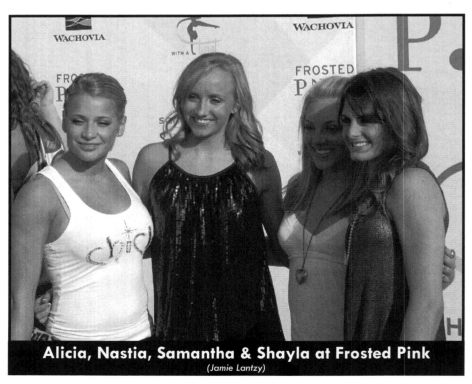

Alicia, Nastia, Samantha & Shayla at Frosted Pink
(Jamie Lantzy)

Ksenia Smenova. The remarkable gymnast quickly shelved her disappointment and delivered a strong beam performance. As Nastia signed autographs for her adoring fans, her first place finish flashed on the scoreboard. She immediately ran to her father for a congratulatory hug.

"I wanted to prove to everyone that I'm still a good beam worker," Nastia said. "I wanted to go out there and show I can make a good beam routine and be on top of the world."

More impressively, Nastia's gold on the beam was her ninth world medal overall. That achievement tied her with Shannon Miller as the American with the most world championship medals.

"To have nine world medals, I can't really believe it," the stunned teenager commented after the competition.

After a long, grueling year, Nastia finished the 2007 season on a high note. Not only had she reestablished herself as a serious all-around competitor, she left the world championships with two gold medals and a silver one to boot!

With the 2008 Olympic Games less than a year away, Nastia seemed back on track, ready to take on the world. She felt healthy and more confident than she had in years. Bring on, Beijing!

"It would be a dream come true just being able to say that I was on the Olympic team."

Chapter 10
Olympic Buildup

At long last the Beijing Olympic season had arrived. On March 1st, the competitive year began with the Tyson American Cup at Madison Square Garden in New York City. Gymnastics legends, like Nadia Comaneci and Mary Lou Retton, sat in the stands, anxiously awaiting the start of the all-important season.

Nastia faced friend Shawn Johnson for the first of what would be many exciting matchups that season. Their friendly rivalry, highlighted by their drastically different styles, had quickly enchanted fans and media alike.

Nastia looked relaxed and confident throughout the debut competition. She delivered strong performances on all four apparatuses. When the final results flashed on the scoreboard, she had won the all-around competition. The normally reserved gymnast felt thrilled with the outcome. She immediately grabbed her cell phone and called her mother to celebrate.

"I'm extremely excited, and I couldn't be happier, especially here in Madison Square Garden," she gushed afterwards. "It's an honor to be here. Just to win, it really feels amazing."

Despite her important victory, though, Nastia remained her biggest critic. She still saw plenty of room for improvement before the Olympics.

"There are always little things to improve upon, and I'm always striving for perfection," she remarked.

Several months later, a rejuvenated Nastia traveled to historic Boston, Massachusetts, for the 2008 U.S. Championships. In what was becoming a tradition, she battled Shawn for the all-around crown. In the end, Nastia finished with the silver medal, although she did outscore her rival on day two of the competition. All in all, she felt quite pleased with her efforts.

"I felt so pumped up and ready to do my best," she stated. "I'm very excited with the outcome."

"I'm just excited to be back," she added with a smile. "It's been a great start to the year so far, and hopefully it will just keep going in that direction."

Marta Karolyi and USA Gymnastics would name six women to the Beijing gymnastics team. The first and second place finishers at the 2008 Olympic Trials in Philadelphia automatically earned spots. The four remaining slots would be decided at a camp selection.

Nastia wanted to nab her ticket to Beijing right off the bat. She arrived in the City of Brotherly Love intent on a top two finish and it showed. She performed brilliantly throughout the Olympic trials and finished the competition in second place behind Shawn.

In a special ceremony following the competition, Nastia and Shawn stood proudly in their Team USA warm-up uniforms. The giddy teenagers grinned ear to ear as they were officially named to the Olympic team.

"These athletes are shining stars for our country as we head into Beijing for the 2008 Olympic Games," Steve Penney, President of USA Gymnastics, announced to an excited crowd.

"It's my great privilege and pleasure to introduce two members of the 2008 U.S. Olympic team: Shawn Johnson and Nastia Liukin."

"We made it," Shawn mouthed to an emotional Nastia, who held back tears. Then they stepped forward and waved to the cheering crowd.

"I'm still in shock right now," an elated Nastia later commented. "It's like a dream come true."

"*I try to set myself apart from the other gymnasts,
and my style is a little bit different
from all the others.*"

Chapter 11
In Demand

The weeks leading up to the Olympics were hectic ones for Nastia filled with interviews, photo shoots and training. Everyone wanted to talk to the new Olympian.

Two months before Beijing, Nastia received a huge honor when she, Shawn and Alicia signed an endorsement deal with CoverGirl makeup. They became the first female athletes ever chosen as the face of the cosmetics company.

CoverGirl spokespeople explained that they chose the girls for their fresh, natural beauty. The trio joined such other CoverGirl models like Queen Latifah, Rihanna and Christie Brinkley.

Nastia felt thrilled to represent CoverGirl. After all, she used the makeup line all the time!

"My favorite beauty product is CoverGirl's Lash Blast mascara. I love using it for competition because it really makes your eyes stand out," she remarked. "My other favorite is Amaze Mint Lipgloss. It gives your lips a little tingle!"

Around the same time, Shawn experienced a serious training crisis when a severe rainstorm flooded her gym. Concerned for her friend, Nastia immediately texted the Iowa native to see if she needed anything.

"I just wanted to make sure you were safe and I'm sorry to hear about the flooding," she wrote. "I hope everything's

OK. Let me know if there's anything we can do. I know we're far away but I'm here for you."

"Thanks. We found a good gym in town but thanks for the support," Shawn replied. "I don't think it's hit everyone yet. Just really surprising. Can't wait to see everybody in a few days. Love you."

Meanwhile, video game fans were sure to see a lot of Nastia over the next few months. Sega® chose the gymnast, along with swimmer Amanda Beard, sprinter Tyson Gay and shot putter Reese Hoffa, to appear on the cover of their game, *Beijing 2008™ - The Official Video Game of the Olympic Games*. The game featured over 35 simulated events from the Olympics.

"These talented individuals epitomize what it is to be an Olympic athlete and we are extremely excited to have them grace the cover of our *Beijing 2008™* video game," said Sean Ratcliffe, SEGA's VP of Marketing.

Growing up with the full-time demands of school and gymnastics, Nastia hadn't played many video games in her life. Yet when SEGA offered to preview the game for the gymnast, she jumped at the chance. The elite athlete had great fun playing the gymnastics game and marveled at how the gymnast in the video performed many of the same bars elements that she did!

"It was a huge honor to be asked to be one of the cover athletes," Nastia gushed. "After playing it and watching everyone play it, it's a huge excitement. I can't wait for it to come out."

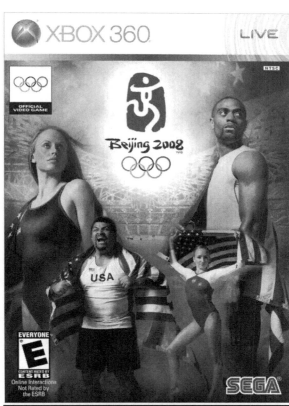

"I definitely need to practice a lot more to be more successful at the game and get higher scores," she added with a laugh.

Nastia on *Beijing 2008* Video Game
(SEGA)

"I do gymnastics for myself.
I want to be one of the best gymnasts in the world."

Chapter 12
Beijing

When Nastia arrived in Beijing, China, she carried a piece of home with her. Because the focused athlete needed proper sleep and sufficient rest to perform at her best, she brought her own pillow and blanket with her. The personal items comforted her greatly.

Nastia then walked around the Olympic Village. She had never seen so many athletes in one place at one time. Among the celebrities she felt most excited to meet? German basketball player Dirk Nowitzki. The star-struck gymnast excitedly introduced herself to the Dallas Maverick and even took a picture with him!

On one of her first days in Beijing, Nastia needed some cash. When she visited an ATM to withdraw money, she saw her picture on the machine! Written in Chinese characters, as well as in English, were the words: destiny.

"Immediately, I felt a big burst of energy, and I felt confident and ready to compete," she later recalled.

Nastia was pleased to discover that she would room with Shawn for the duration of the Olympics. Although many found the arrangement strange, considering the girls were each other's top rival for the all-around gold, both teenagers dismissed any notions of awkwardness. Besides, they were more focused on their first competition, the team event.

As the reigning world champions, the American ladies entered the Beijing Olympics as favorites to take the team title. Nastia and Shawn, America's star gymnasts, were joined by: Chellsie Memmel, Alicia Sacramone, Samantha Peszek and Bridget Sloan.

Meanwhile, a cloud of doubt, regarding the true age of three gymnasts, hung over the Chinese team. A few months earlier, *Xinhua*, the Chinese government's news agency, and *China Daily* newspaper, both reported gymnast He Kexin's age as thirteen. Many believed that key members of the Chinese Gymnastics Federation had created false passports for He and two other gymnasts, so the exceptionally talented girls could compete in Beijing.

Because the Chinese were the U.S. women's chief threat for team gold, the media bombarded them with questions regarding the age controversy. However, the Americans refused to get swept up in the brewing scandal. Instead, they merely replied that they were focused only on their own performances.

Shortly before the competition began, the U.S. team received a serious blow when both Chellsie and Samantha went down with injuries. Doctors only cleared the girls to compete on bars, so the rest of the team scurried to adjust to new lineups.

At the end of night one, the girls sat in second place behind the strong Chinese team. While they weren't sparkling, committing a few mistakes here and there, they delivered strong routines.

"We've been over here a week, training, training, training. Our team doctor said we were like a bunch of racehorses, we were so ready to get out there," Nastia remarked afterwards. "We wanted to compete, and I think everybody might have had some extra nerves."

On night two, the American women looked off for the last half of the competition. In fact, each girl received costly deductions on their final apparatus, the floor exercise. Meanwhile, to the home country crowd's delight, the Chinese team rallied with many powerful performances. In the end, they won gold, the U.S. took silver and Romania claimed bronze.

"We didn't have the healthiest team this year so that made it a little harder but we all fought for each other," Nastia remarked. "We just wanted to do it for each of us and to hopefully make our country proud."

"I definitely have no regrets," she continued. "I'm happy with how everything went and to say that you have an Olympic medal is just amazing."

With the team event now in the record books, the focus turned toward the all-around competition. Nearly every news outlet and gymnastics expert agreed that Nastia and Shawn were the top two contenders for the title.

"They are such totally different gymnasts," Kim Zmeskal, the first American woman to win the world all-around title, told the *Los Angeles Times*. "Shawn is great on the power events, the floor and the vault. Nastia is so good on the uneven

Team USA Wins Olympic Silver
(Getty Images)

bars and balance beam. It almost seems as if you like one or the other."

The fact that both girls were good friends who represented the same country added intrigue to the duel. Except Nastia and Shawn genuinely liked each other and never engaged in any trash talk.

"People just can't believe that we can be so competitive and at the same time we can still be such good friends," Nastia commented. "But we are friends."

"We're really good friends, we're really good competitors and we're both really good gymnasts," Shawn agreed.

In addition, the girls always expressed admiration for one another's gymnastics. Each had unique qualities that the other gymnast admired.

"I'd love to do [Nastia's] uneven bars. Her one-handed swings, wow," Shawn told the *Los Angeles Times*.

"[Shawn's] doing two and a half twists on her vault," Nastia said. "I'd like to have that."

Tickets for the ladies all-around competition were a hot commodity. In fact, people were so desperate to see the event that some even produced counterfeit tickets!

One person not in attendance? Anna Liukin. Nastia's mother always suffered a strong case of nerves when her daughter competed and preferred to spend time away from the arena during competition. Instead, she nervously checked her phone every few minutes for updates. The all-around event was no exception for Nastia's mom who, before the competition, texted her daughter, "Stay focused and have fun!! Text me when you're done. Love you."

Wearing her favorite color, pink, Nastia began the competition on her weakest event, vault. She could not have performed a better one. Her form was perfect and she stuck her landing with commanding confidence.

The focused competitor competed next on her two best events. The eighteen-year-old gave a thrilling bars performance packed with difficulty. She followed that with a remarkable balance beam routine that highlighted her superb form, amazing flexibility and unparalleled artistry.

Now sitting in first place, Nastia ended her all-around competition with the floor exercise. Performing to the Russian piece, "Dark Eyes," Nastia's exquisite musical interpretation set her miles apart from the other gymnasts, while her tumbling appeared light and effortless. When she finished her routine, the elated athlete smiled brightly and ran to embrace her father.

Nastia and Shawn in the Olympic All-Around
(Getty Images)

"That could be a routine that we are watching for generations," declared *NBC* commentator Al Trautwig.

In the end, Nastia won the all-around gold medal. She had done it! The determined gymnast had accomplished a lifelong dream. Upon learning the news, the normally reserved competitor broke down in tears.

The giddy teenager then excitedly grabbed her cell phone. After all, she had a very important text to send.

"I won," the new Olympic champion texted to Anna. "Love you, Mom."

Meanwhile, Shawn won the silver medal, and China's Yang Yilin took bronze. The runner-up had nothing but praise for the winner.

"I gave my heart and soul out there today," a gracious Shawn said. "Nastia deserved the gold."

Throughout the medal ceremony, Nastia looked overwhelmed with her momentous achievement. She shed tears as her country's national anthem played while the American flag was raised.

"Standing on the podium and hearing `Olympic champion' next to my name was a dream come true," she remarked afterwards. "Everything pays off at this very moment."

Meanwhile, Valeri told a reporter, "It's not possible to describe how proud I am."

"It makes it so sweet knowing that I've been through so much with injuries and doubters," Nastia said. "But it made me stronger and made me the person I am today. It's been a long journey, but it's been worth it."

Nastia also remembered how close her father had come to all-around gold at the 1988 Olympics. She hoped her triumph would ease some of her dad's disappointment from twenty years earlier.

"Just to know that he was so close to (the all-around gold) and didn't quite achieve it," she said. " I hope I cleared away those bad little memories for him. I hope that this definitely tops it."

With the all-around title securely in her pocket, Nastia still had the opportunity to win even more Olympic medals. She qualified for three event finals: uneven bars, balance beam and floor exercise.

The floor exercise competition took place on a Sunday. Dressed in a striking red leotard, Nastia delivered another wonderful floor routine punctuated by her maturity and grace.

At the end of the event, she won her third Olympic medal, the bronze, behind Romanian Sandra Izbasa's gold and Shawn's silver.

"I have a collection (of medals) now, which is really cool," she remarked happily.

Nastia turned her attention toward the uneven bars next. Perhaps her strongest event, she hoped to capture a fourth medal.

He Kexin led off the uneven bars finals. She gave an exciting performance with many difficult skills and scored a 16.725. Nastia followed with an equally strong routine with several difficult release skills. In the end, she also scored a 16.725. Because the International Olympic Committee forbids sports from awarding duplicate medals, the International Gymnastics Federation created several tiebreakers in their scoring system. In the end, Nastia lost the gold on the second tiebreaker.

"I am a little disappointed," Nastia later commented. "I tied. It wasn't that I got second by three-tenths or five-tenths. I had the same exact score, and that is what makes it harder to take. But unfortunately, you can't control the judges."

"I have one more day, and I would like to finish my Olympics on a high note," she added.

On Nastia's final day of Olympic competition, she faced the balance beam. Wearing a pretty white leotard, she gave a solid, fluid performance. When she landed her dismount, the ecstatic teenager broke into a wide grin. Whatever happened with the judges, she had ended her Olympic experience with another clean routine.

Nastia's strong score of 16.025 placed her second overall. With her fifth medal of the games, she tied legend Shannon Miller in the record books for most medals won by an American gymnast at the Olympics.

"To say I have five medals at my first Olympic Games means the world to me," Nastia commented. "And just having one gold is OK, because it's the one that means the most."

A jubilant Shawn, who had stood on the second step of the podium three times, took home the gold medal, while Fei Cheng finished third. Always a classy competitor, Nastia felt genuinely thrilled for her friend and teammate.

"I was pulling for her," she smiled. "[Shawn] finally got that gold. She deserved it 100%."

Later that night, after Nastia and Shawn re-turned to their

Olympic All-Around Champion
(Getty Images)

room, they stayed up until two in the morning! The two teenagers chatted and shared their thoughts on their Olympic experiences until exhaustion eventually set in and they drifted off to sleep. They felt enormously grateful, not only for their multitude of medals, but because a very good friend accompanied them on their priceless Olympic journey.

When looking back on her Olympic highlights, Nastia stressed that her victory was a group effort. Her achievements were not just her's alone.

"Going into the Olympics, it was exactly twenty years from when my dad competed, so just to be there with him, it was very emotional," she stated. "Winning the gold medal, it wasn't just for me, it was for my dad, it was for my mom, and everyone back in the states. Knowing that made me really emotional."

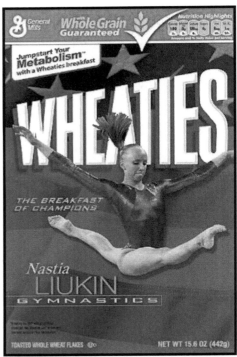

Nastia Poses with her Wheaties box.
(General Mills)

"*I missed being in the gym.
I missed training.
I missed having something to feel like
I had a fulfilling day.*"

Chapter 13
A Star

When Nastia returned home from Beijing, her hometown of Parker, Texas, organized a parade in her honor. Thousands turned out to cheer for their golden girl as she rode down the route in a pink convertible.

"I wasn't expecting this many people," she said later, when addressing the crowd. "Thank you all so much for being here tonight. It's a very special night for me. It feels so great to be home."

Nastia also received exciting news when she learned that General Mills had selected her to grace the front of their Wheaties box. She and American decathlete Bryan Clay were the only two athletes chosen from the Beijing Games.

"Every young athlete aspires to one day see their face on the cover of the Wheaties box," Nastia said. "It's been a huge inspiration to see great gymnastics champions on the box, like Mary Lou and Carly, plus the 'Magnificent Seven' from 1996. It's a privilege and an honor for me to be on the box, and I'm very excited to be part of the Wheaties tradition."

"I tell young athletes all the time that if you want to become a champion, you need to stay focused, train hard, and pay attention to what you eat," the role model added.

Nastia's exciting opportunities also extended toward the clothing industry. The denim company, Vanilla Star, signed her to design and endorse jeans for their clothing line.

"We feel that Nastia is special, not only for her amazing skills but as a role model and inspiration to young generations," Vanilla Star president Mark Levy stated.

"I am really excited to be part of Vanilla Star's Smart Girls Rock ad campaign," Nastia gushed. "I know what it is like to have a dream in your mind and work as hard as you can to achieve it. I'm just happy I can encourage others to do the same."

Nastia also embarked on whirlwind bookings on the talk show circuit. She met Oprah, chatted with Barbara Walters and Whoopi Goldberg on *The View* and joked with Jay Leno and Conan O'Brien.

A few months after the Olympics, Nastia also headlined the *Tour of Gymnastics Superstars* which played 37 major arenas throughout the United States. The cast included a bevy of gymnastics legends like: Shawn Johnson, Shannon Miller and Paul Hamm.

To the crowd's delight, Nastia and Shawn appeared at the beginning of the evening to introduce them to their show. Sometimes, Nastia had to wait for the cheers to die down so she could finish speaking her intro!

Dressed in red, white and blue, Nastia held a microphone as she addressed the screaming crowd by saying, "Tonight you're going to be entertained by Olympians from the Beijing Games, other Olympic games, and you'll hear some great music as well, as we kick off the *Tour of Gymnastics Superstars!*"

Every night, Nastia performed a touching balance beam routine dedicated to her father set to Bob Carlisle's "Butterfly Kisses." Dressed in a two-piece hot pink outfit, she also unveiled a spunky bars program to Saving Jane's "Super Girl." Her beautiful artistry was then displayed in an elegant floor routine.

Nastia also had fun appearing on several popular television shows, even landing a bit role on her favorite TV drama, *Gossip Girl*. The in-demand teen also filmed stints on *Make It or Break It*, *The Biggest Loser* and *Hellcats*.

Perhaps the most exciting news occurred when Nastia launched the Nastia Liukin Supergirl Cup, a competition celebrating young, rising, non-elite female gymnasts. The Olympic champion felt humbled and honored to see her name attached to a major gymnastics event. She also felt excited to promote female empowerment to young girls.

"The Supergirl brand defines that attitude of do what you love to do," Nastia remarked to the *Associated Press*. "It's making good decisions outside of school. Who you're friends with, the decisions you make. But it's also the empowerment of doing what you love to do and being confident in yourself."

"Who knows if this will be their last experience with gymnastics. Or it could be a great first step to the rest of their careers," she continued. "Even if they never make that leap (to elite gymnastics), to know they competed this one year and got that experience and got to be on that stage...it's a huge spotlight."

In addition, the major department store, J.C. Penney, unveiled a Supergirl by Nastia clothing line. The trendy, affordable clothing stressed the message of empowerment, creativity, strength, intelligence and independence.

"I am so proud to present the Supergirl by Nastia line, which I believe represents not only a fashionable and affordable option, but also communicates an important message of empowerment," Nastia said.

The Olympic champion loved inspiring younger generations. After all, as a young girl, she, too, looked up to certain athletes. In particular, she admired athletes like Lilia Podkopayeva, Svetlana Khorkina and Lance Armstrong.

So when *Beacon Street Girls*, a popular book series aimed at the junior high crowd, asked her to be their celebrity role model for their new social networking site, she jumped at the opportunity. At the popular website, fans left messages for Nastia and asked her questions about a variety of issues.

"Club BSG is important to how I connect with my fans," Nastia remarked. "Through the gymnastics team on the site, I have the ability to reach even more girls than ever before! On the site, we will be talking about self-esteem and staying fit through positive life choices."

Nastia never strayed far from the gymnastics community, though. Valued for her years of competitive experience, USA Gymnastics offered her a role on the selection committee for international events. The Olympic champion began working with Marta Karolyi to help monitor and select the best gymnasts for international assignments.

Of course, any time Nastia showed up to a competition to assess the girls' progress, people asked if she planned to return to competition. She always answered honestly. She had no idea!

However, in late 2011, Nastia suddenly began experiencing the itch to compete again. She missed the daily grind of training and the thrill of competition. But did she have the drive in her to attempt a comeback?

Nastia began dropping hints to her father that she might return to competitive gymnastics. Valeri, however, wasn't sure how truly committed his daughter was to a comeback.

Before long, Nastia began showing up to the gym putting in daily training sessions. Valeri watched his only child thoughtfully. She logged hard-working hours without any prompting from him. He knew that his focused daughter was serious about her return.

Nastia Performs to "Butterfly Kisses"
(Amy Jeanius)

In October of 2011, thanks to her role with USA Gymnastics, Nastia traveled with the American team to the World Championships in Tokyo, Japan. She watched the competition carefully, yearning to be on the floor competing with the other girls. It was at these championships that Nastia announced her intent to train for the 2011 London Olympics.

I think that I just owe it to myself to try, to give it another shot," she told the *Associated Press*. "I'm 100 percent committed to trying to make this dream of mine come true."

"There's nothing guaranteed," she added. "The only promise that I can make is to give 100 percent and see where it takes me."

Of course, the gymnastics world welcomed Nastia back with open arms. The sport missed her unbelievable technique, beautiful gymnastics and classy sportsmanship.

Nastia's Supergirl Clothing Line

Whatever happened in her second Olympic bid, though, Nastia had already left an indelible mark on her sport. She would always be remembered as one of its brightest and most admired competitors.

"For me, Beijing was more of a destiny," she said. "London would be more like a dream."

A dream for Nastia and her legions of fans.

WOGA's Golden Girl
(Joseph Dzidrums)

Ballerina on the Beam
(Ricardo Bufolin)

Essential Links

Nastia's Official Website
www.NastiaLiukin.com

Nastia's Twitter Account
www.twitter.com/#!/NastiaLiukin

SuperGirl's Official Website
www.supergirl.com

USA Gymnastics
www.usagym.org

GymnStars
www.GymnStars.com

Author Website
www.ChristineDzidrums.com

Ricardo Bufolin's Photography
www.flickr.com/photos/ricardobufolin

GymBox
www.gymbox.net

Nastia Liukin

About the Author

Christine Dzidrums holds a bachelor's degree in Theater Arts from California State University, Fullerton. She previously wrote the biographies: *Joannie Rochette: Canadian Ice Princess, Yuna Kim: Ice Queen, Shawn Johnson: Gymnastics' Golden Girl* and *Nastia Liukin: Ballerina of Gymnastics*. Her first novel, *Cutters Don't Cry*, won a 2010 Moonbeam Children's Book Award in the Young Adult Fiction category. She also wrote the tween book, *Fair Youth*, and the beginning reader books, *Timmy and the Baseball Birthday Party* and *Timmy Adopts a Girl Dog*. Christine also authored the picture book, *Princess Dessabelle Makes a Friend*. She recently competed her second novel, *Kaylee: The 'What If?' Game.*

BUILD YOUR SKATESTARS™ COLLECTION TODAY!

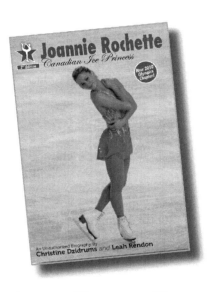

At the 2010 Vancouver Olympics, tragic circumstances thrust **Joannie Rochette** into the international spotlight when her beloved mother died two days before the ladies short program. The world held their breath for the bereaved figure skater when she opted to compete in her mom's memory. Joannie then captured hearts everywhere when she courageously skated two moving programs to win the Olympic bronze medal. *Joannie Rochette: Canadian Ice Princess* reveals answers to ice skating enthusiasts' most asked questions.

Meet figure skating's biggest star: **Yuna Kim**. The Korean trailblazer produced two legendary performances at the 2010 Vancouver Olympic Games to win the gold medal in convincing fashion. *Yuna Kim: Ice Queen*, the second book in the **Skate Stars** series, uncovers the compelling story of how the beloved figure skater overcame poor training conditions, various injuries and numerous other obstacles to become world and Olympic champion.

BUILD YOUR GYMNSTARS™ COLLECTION TODAY!

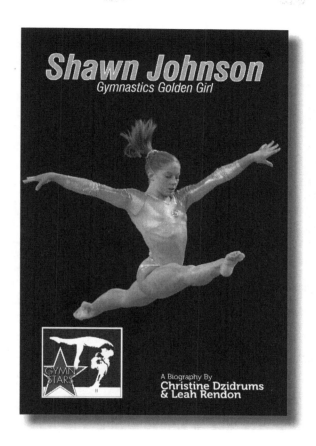

Shawn Johnson, the young woman from Des Moines, Iowa, captivated the world at the 2008 Beijing Olympics when she snagged a gold medal on the balance beam.

Shawn Johnson: Gymnastics' Golden Girl, the first volume in the **GymnStars** series, chronicles the life and career of one of sport's most beloved athletes.

Also From

2010 Moonbeam Children's Book Award Winner! In a series of raw journal entries written to her absentee father, a teenager chronicles her penchant for self-harm, a serious struggle with depression and an inability to vocally express her feelings.

"I play the 'What If?'" game all the time. It's a cruel, wicked game."

Meet free spirit Kaylee Matthews, the most popular girl in school. But when the teenager suffers a devastating loss, her sunny personality turns dark as she struggles with debilitating panic attacks and unresolved anger. Can Kaylee repair her broken spirit, or will she forever remain a changed person?

Meet Princess Dessabelle, a spoiled, lonely princess with a quick temper. When she orders a kind classmate to be her friend, she learns the true meaning of friendship.

Made in the USA
Middletown, DE
10 December 2015